The Street of Perfect Love

THE STREET OF PERFECT LOVE

JULIAN STANNARD

First published in 2014 by
Worple Press
Achill Sound, 2b Dry Hill Road
Tonbridge
Kent TN9 1LX.
www.worplepress.co.uk

Cover image by Dan Harley

Printed by imprintdigital
Upton Pyne, Exeter
www.imprintdigital.net

Typeset by narrator
www.narrator.me.uk
info@narrator.me.uk
033 022 300 39

ISBN: 978-1-905208-27-2

Acknowledgements

Some of these poems have appeared in the *TLS, Poetry Review, Manhattan Review, Ambit, Poetry, Salamander, Spectator* and *A Mutual Friend: Poems for Charles Dickens* (Two Rivers Press, 2012). 'September 1939' appears in *The Best of British Poetry 2014* (Salt).

One Night

[...]

And there on that ordinary, plain bed
I had love's body, knew those intoxicating lips,
red and sensual,
red lips so intoxicating
that now as I write, after so many years,
in my lonely house, I'm drunk with passion again.

Cavafy, *Collected Poems*

For Jack and William

Contents

Chastity

Although I'd long sunk
into Jim's unwashed sheets
finding myself in a state of
existence known as sleeping
I was conscious of a dark shape
clanking glasses which
turned out to be none other
than Jim himself who didn't
like to drink alone but who
would if there was no one
around to oblige him.
How can you sleep like that,
he said, after writing
a poem of that strange ilk?
And he recited the poem to me
which contained the words:
slipping off into the far corners
of the metropolitana.

Jim, I said, it's the middle of
the night and tomorrow
I must go to the Palace of Justice.
It's because you must go to the Palace of Justice
I'm clanking these glasses, he said.
And he turned on the one functioning
bulb in that unimaginable Profundis.
And we need to talk about that
box of After Eights you gave to Phyllis.
Jim, I said, it was only a box of chocolates.

Well, I've never seen such a phallic box
of chocolates, Jim said, and I said
I've never considered

1

After Eights could be anything other
than a spur to chastity.
Well, said Jim, if you weren't a literary man
I'd beat the shit out of you.

We drank under that naked bulb
till the dawn broke
and Genoese sparrows threw themselves
against the windows, only the windows
were broken so the sparrows
flew in and crapped in the corners.
Jim's head had fallen onto his chest
and I threw a jacket around my shoulders
and ran to the Palace of Justice.

When I got there
I saw that my estranged wife
had attached herself to a megaphone
not that she needed one (at least
that was my view).

Thigh-Slapping on the Riviera

I was at the Town Hall
in Rapallo, trying
to find something out.
The concierge
a man with a moustache
said *Sono ignorante*
non so niente,
I call the Dottoressa.
When the Dottoressa came
she said You must be
our German scholar.
The Dottoressa
linked arms and took me
this way and that way
– her German scholar –
down marble corridors
into painted rooms.

When we met
her colleagues
she said Here is
the German scholar
and as the sun soared
I practised clicking
my heels and found
that it came quite easily:
so I clicked this way
and clicked that way
and clicked across
the courtyard
in front of the mayor
and sometimes I stooped
to kiss a hand,

a lady's hand I ought to add.
We German scholars
like a little hand.

Oh look at the German scholar
(how could I say I was English!)
They wanted a bit of clicking
and my God I was giving it to them.
A click here, a click there
a sudden stoop,
I was reviving the old clicking alliance.
They had their Mare Nostrum,
I had a pair of heels.

Dickens Discovers His Italian Babylon

In the course of two months
the flitting shapes and shadows
of my dismal entering reverie
gradually resolved themselves
into familiar forms and substances

and I already began to think
that when the time should come
for closing the long holiday
and turning back to England
I might part from Genoa with

anything but a glad heart.
It is a place that *grows upon you*
every day. There seems to be
always something to find out.
There are the most extraordinary

alleys and by-ways to walk about in.
You can lose your way (what a comfort
that is, when you are idle!) twenty
times a day. It abounds in
the strangest contrasts: things that

are picturesque, ugly, mean,
magnificent, delightful and offensive
break upon the view at every turn.
The houses are immensely high
painted in all sorts of colours

and are in every stage of damage,
dirt and lack of repair.
As it is impossible for coaches
to penetrate into these streets
there are sedan chairs, gilded

and otherwise, for hire in divers
places. I had earlier made
the mistake of asking the whip
to take me to Piazza San Bernardo.
The young women are not generally

pretty but they walk remarkably well.
I had earlier made the mistake
of asking the whip to take me
to an apothecary. The women are not
generally pretty but oh they walk

remarkably well. How shall I forget
the Streets of Palaces: Strada Nuova
and Via Balbi!: the great, heavy, stone
balconies, one above another, and
tier over tier: with here and there,
one larger than the rest, towering
high up – a huge marble platform;
the doorless vestibules, massively
barred lower windows, immense
public staircases, thick marble pillars,
strong dungeon-like arches, and
dreary, dreaming, echoing vaulted
chambers: among which the eye
wanders again, and again, and again
as every palace is succeeded by another
– the terrace gardens between house
and house, with green arches of

the vine, and groves of orange trees
and blushing oleander in full bloom
twenty, thirty, forty feet above

the street. The steep up-hill streets
of small palaces with marble terraces
looking down into close by-ways –
the magnificent and innumerable
churches; and the rapid passage
from a street of stately edifices
into a maze of the vilest squalor,
steaming with unwholesome stenches
and swarming with half-naked
children and whole worlds of
dirty people – make up, altogether,
such a scene of wonder: so lively
and yet so dead: so noisy and yet
so quiet: so obtrusive, and yet
so shy and lowering: so wide awake
and yet so fast asleep: that is
a sort of intoxication to a stranger
to walk on, and on, and on, and
look about him. A bewildering
phantasmagoria, with all the
inconsistency of a dream and all
the pain and all the pleasure
of an extravagant reality!

I made the mistake of asking
the whip to take me
to Vico dell' Amor Perfetto.
The women are not generally
pretty but oh but oh but oh
they do walk remarkably well.

Lorsica

When the storm came
they were taken out of themselves
and no one saw that the boys
had gone up with the cows
and when night fell you could see
torchlight on the slopes of Ramaceto

and they were saying they would
find them cowering and safe
and when they got to the stone house
they found the boys had been struck
by lightning and the cows were dead too
and Enzo shouted across the valley
Morti, i ragazzi sono morti!

and Gabriella who had waited
for her sons to return from the war
only to have them killed
on the slopes of Ramaceto
started to scream and the valley
explored every angle of her grief

and when the sun rose there were olives
and grapes and there were drooling dogs
and Angelo and Fillipo were yellow birds
gripping the tiles of their mother's roof

Winston and Candy

I was walking along the banks of the River Yangtze
suffused with delicious feelings of cherry blossom.
Winston gripped my elbow and whispered,
Candy, one day we could put down a deposit on a horse.
My heart skipped and I was giddy enough to kiss him!

I am Candy and Winston has dreams of being my lover.
He is as loyal as a dog and I can't tell you how ugly he is.
I'm going to talk about China's over-heated horse market.
Foreigners scatter their money. Macroeconomics!
Chairman Deng said getting rich was glorious.

Big horse, little horse, who gives a fuck about mice.
Kung says, I love my wife, I love my horse, my horse is quiet.
I told Winston, Change your reading habits, *exercise!*
Affordable horses are on the decline! People are marching.
We are millions! I hear horses cantering over the plains.

What is that sound high in the air? Genghis? Buddha?
Now the government is restricting horse credit.
You keep a horse five years, you pay less tax.
You buy two horses, they throw your baby in the lake.
The unflinching discipline of our revolving emperors!

Stations of the Cross

Someone had taken an axe
to my life which meant
that although everything
was in pieces we needed
a Christmas tree
if only for the children
to gather round as they listened
to a wound-up version of
Stille Nacht, Heilige Nacht.

Someone had taken an axe
to the forest – now there were
Christmas trees throughout the city.
Lucky me! I took myself
to the Mercato Orientale
to pick up my tree
and screw down the thorns
because someone had
taken an axe to my life.

I picked up my Christmas tree
and carried it all the way
to our house on the hill
which had turned into
an outpost of hell but
even hell wants a Christmas tree
UN ALBERO DI NATALE.

I carried my tree
past the Hotel Metropoli
I carried my tree
to Saint Anna's Funicular.
Oh, they said,

it's St. Julian the leper
Julian of the *mot juste*
Julian with an axe in his head
carrying a Christmas tree
to an outpost of hell.

Sometimes people swung
a punch
just for the hell of it.
Someone started hammering
a nail into my head
just for the hell of it.
Evidently
I had done something wrong!
Then I carried my tree along
Corso Magenta where the blind man
        turned a blind eye.

And I carried my tree
up Salita Santa Maria della Sanità
and I carried my tree to the eighth floor
because the lift was broken
and the woman who'd taken an axe
to my life said, Ah, un albero di natale
we've been waiting so fucking long
for un albero di natale.

Put it there in the corner.
Careful, careful.
Oh look it's beautiful,
a little red perhaps
but beautiful. Here's a cloth
to wipe your face.
You'll frighten the children.
They'll think you've gone mad.

Via Monte Bello

The lampshade
hanging from

the ceiling
is Eleanor

of Acquitaine
kneeling

La Baia di Silenzio

I lay myself down
in the Bay of Silence.
The wind kicked up
and scudded across
the sea. The wind
got into the rigging
and the Bay of Silence
wasn't silent at all
with sails flapping
like scarecrows
on the threshold of
delirium. A girl
shrieked. Something
was coming off
the sea which
could only be death
or the sister of death
or the cocktail of
death or the methadone
of death or the
ecstasy of death
or the aftershave
of death or the sweet
morning feeling
of death, or the hit me,
hit me, hit me
of death, or the *la la la*
of death. Goodbye.

Minestrone

When I telephone
my erstwhile innamorata
she speaks in the voice
of minestrone. Not the minestrone
her mother would make
having stood the entire morning
in a small windowless kitchen
throwing diced vegetables
into a pot whilst intoning
Giacomo Leopardi's
'The Approach of Death'.

No, it is not that voice.
Nor does the voice say:
I could rustle up a scallopina,
some grilled aubergines
and a salad so fresh and delectable
you would glow, mio caro, you would glow!

No, the voice is the voice
of a minestrone hunkering down
at the bottom of the pot:
it's thick and beginning to congeal
it will probably do for another day.

I could warm it up, *mio caro bello*,
and scrape it out with a spoon
and serve it to you in a bowl
whose hair-line crack has formed
two distinct geographical kingdoms.
I could do all of this for you
because once upon a time ·
do you remember? – you were my husband.

Via Antonio Burlando

Don't go there. Not today:
October 11th, when the sky
is as thick as a minestrone
you would never want to eat
even if you were feeling peckish.

Tell me why I'm in this flat
in Via Antonio Burlando
where every chandelier
         has a single bulb.

I'm standing on the poggiolo
letting the rain drench me.
Rain – that schoolboy ballad
which Edward Thomas sang.
He heard the Angel of Death
in that frozen barracks. Mud on
his boots, Ovaltine comforter.

I'm eight floors up. I could die
in a moment. I could throw
myself into the River Bisagno
which is a river without water
whose occupants are rats
         the size of horses.

I can see the stadium
         the prison
             the necropolis.

And they smoke when they deal the cards
in the bars of Via Antonio Burlando
ignoring the VIETATO FUMARE

the butcher serving nerve ends
Colonel Burlando bright-eyed on the night bus.
The Farmacia sells only suppositories.
The fishmonger can get hold of a fish
which will send us into ecstasies.

October 12th, the colour of the city has changed.
With a little eye-stretching you can
see the sea hovering below the sky:
Via Antonio Burlando, we're on the
offal side of the city, valleys break
into the hinterland, a police siren has
replaced the sound of rain. I'm eight floors
up smoking a cigarette on a poggiolo
                    which shakes in the wind.

Napoli

The boat was beating across the bay,
we had our backs to Vesuvius,
the wind smacked our faces.
Naples was an enormous packet of cigarettes
you could smoke until you conked out:
the cigarettes were never going to run out
and nor was the coffee, the drugs,
the prostitutes, the locked churches,
the scooters, the rice cakes, the evil eye,
the boys called Gennaro, the funiculars,
the shrines to Madonna, the shrines
to Maradona, the bullet holes, the heat,
the permanent state of crucifixion.
Anyone could be crucified two thousand
years ago but to be crucified now
to be crucified in Napoli – lift me up!

The Necropolis

When I walked into the necropolis
at Genoa I saw that every grave

had been allocated a panettone
and because the Council was in

broad terms a coalition of the left
every panettone was in a red box

and because every panettone
was in a red box I had a hunch

the old Maoist–Leninist–Stalinist
front were calling a meeting

with the dead and because the
dead were bored of being dead

they clapped and shouted
like nuns who have discovered

the libido and because nuns
have discovered the libido

I am going to bring the poem
to a sudden end. Sleep well!

Buddhism

After years of silence
my ex-wife sends me
a salami through the post.

I have to sign for it
and then I take it
into the flat and put it

in the fridge. And then I remember
a Calabrian neighbour
who hung his salamis

in every room in the house.
He was a doctor, or had at least
acquired some kind of

medical qualification –
no luck finding a job.
He practised Buddhism

and this endowed him
with patience and good feelings
especially towards the salamis

which, it has to be said, gave
the apartment a particular aroma.
 I like to keep my hand in,

he said. And he took out
a knife and began to chop the salami
in the hallway. I take my ex-wife's

salami out of the fridge and spend
much of the day looking at it.
Years of silence and then a salami!

And I look for a sharp knife
and slice off a piece which,
a little nervously, I eat. Delicious.

King's Cross

When I lived in King's Cross
I used to lie on the bed and listen
to my bones melting. At first
I thought I was listening to Elgar
and then I thought I was listening
to the couple who'd moved
into the flat above and who were
getting to know each other better
and then I thought I was listening
to the music of the spheres.
I was listening to my bones melting.

Hampshire

When you drive me
into Hampshire
it always seems
you're taking me to bed:

a king-sized bed
involving vast amounts
of goose feather!

When you drive me
into Hampshire
cows stand in the mist

and swans loop on the river.
Let's stop the car!
Let's find a glade,

a cavalry of blue bells.
I'll make the crook
of my arm into a pillow.

Jerry Hall Meets Salvador Dalí

I flew to Paris at seventeen
and got talking to Jean-Paul
Sartre and Simone de Beauvoir
over coffee. I was happy
to meet them. The trouble is,
I just can't write poems
when I'm happy.

Mother said, The Riviera
is the place to go.
I bought a pink bikini,
some high-heeled shoes
and walked myself along the beach.

I love cooking, I love gardening.
I keep chickens. Mick's an alley cat.
Happy, happy, mostly happy.

Salvador Dalí said,
Why don't you run naked
through my sculpture garden?

Burlington Arcade

I'm being carried down
the Burlington Arcade
by Beadles in top hats,
jewellers on both sides
holding out their hands
and wrapped in cashmere.
When people speak of
near-death experiences
they're always going through
tunnels, they're happy,
they're never going through
the Burlington Arcade.

Eric says, It's good
to see you wearing clothes
and I have to admit he's
wearing the most beautiful
trousers and I say, Eric
you're not supposed to be
in this poem. Get back
into your shop! I can see
a light at the end of the tunnel.
The Head Beadle's saying
'Burlington Gardens!'

Should I tip him?
Am I dead?
What happens next?

Aldgate East

I loved fucking in Aldgate East:
the gap in the curtain letting in
the light from Whitechapel,
your buttocks almost perfect.
Don't stop, you said, don't stop.
I won't, I said, you needn't worry
about that, no stopping for a while:
a good service to Aldgate East.
Appetite, appetite, no end to it.
Most days slip into oblivion
somehow it's different in Aldgate East.
Your body seems to glow.
Let's change direction, let's make it
better than it is already. Ok, you said.
Are you happy? Yes! It steals up
unexpectedly. Oh, I'm happy too.
Aldgate East, all give, all take.

September 1939

London seems peaceful
and somehow rather empty.
I think we're going to be okay
I'm feeling almost happy.
I think we should get married
or have some kind of affair.
I think we should have a holiday:
Devon maybe, can't go to Berlin!
I wonder what they're saying
on the Kurfüstendamm? I'm going
to write to Heinrich and say
this war really shouldn't make
the blindest bit of difference.
Oh, what do you think?
I think we should dress down
and make a habit of undressing
a little more often than we do.
Come, let me help you.
I think we should go to the Ritz
and really splash out.
I think we should pretend
we can't sleep because
the nightingales won't leave us
in peace. I think we should sing
There'll always be an England
and just when we've got the hang
of it we should suddenly stop
and look embarrassed.

I think we should bruise our
mouths with damsons.
I think we should listen to jazz
and move our bodies like this.

I think I'll wear that cardigan
which makes me feel slightly odd.
I think we should go to that restaurant
in Dean Street. I think I'm going
to throw my arms around you
and hold you a little more tightly
than I normally hold you
which will cause you to say,
Please stop, you're hurting me!
I think we should listen to the wireless.
I think we should lie for hours
in a field and look at the sky.

The Gargantuan Muffin Beauty Contest

We were at the Edison Hotel on West 47th Street
for the annual muffin beauty contest –
I can't tell you how pumped up we were.
Times Square was having another psychotic judder.
The bellhop was all thumbs up: Sir, have a nice day
and get one gratis. All those avenues of doors
and the Hispanic chambermaid who couldn't speak English.
Spider-Man was doing all that Spider-Man shit
just to get a bird's eye view. Donna Summer
was almost dead and we were barely into spring.
I want to dance to Love to Love You Baby, I want to groan.
I've never seen so many high quality muffins.
If I wasn't a religious man, and maybe I wasn't
I would have said the muffins were walking on water:
I've never felt so half and half. Have you read the bible?
The bellhop said: You ain't seen muffin yet.
They were drifting in from Queens, Brooklyn, Harlem,
The Bronx, Manhattan muffins too and that weird
cute Coke-faced muffin who'd taken the subway
from Coney Island. If only I were a betting man,
but hey I am a betting man, it's Coney Island every time.
Lou Reed isn't getting any younger. Zappa said
Girl you thought he was a man but he was a muffin,
he hung around till you found he didn't know nuthin.
In the lobby Nina Simone was singing, I loves you Muffin
and in the restroom they piped in Mack the Knife:
Hey Sookie Taudry, Jenny Diver, Polly Peachum
and old Miss Lulu Brown. Muffin The Romance
was the biggest show in town. We were hurtling back
to the 1970s and sometimes the 1970s are almost
as good as the 1930s. I want my muffins to be ahistorical:
shit just to say ahistorical makes me joyful.
I saw Leonard Cohen crooning with a couple

of octogenarian muffins and I'm telling you now
the lobby was pleasantly disturbing. You may find
yourself behind the wheel of a large automobile.
You may find yourself in another part of the world.
You may find yourself at the gargantuan muffin beauty contest
and you may ask yourself, Well, how did I get here?
Times Square was having another psychotic judder.
Love is in the air, it's in the whisper of the trees.
This is not America, this is the cover version:
sun, sex, sin, divine intervention, death and destruction,
welcome to The Sodom and Gomorrah Show.
All those white muffins trying to be black muffins!
Give us our daily muffin, save us from temptation.
Jimmy Buffet was singing, Why don't we get drunk
and screw? In Times Square the most beautiful muffins
in the world were hanging on a thousand screens.
Where are my singing Tibetan balls? Am I dead?

Miss Pinkerton

Sometimes I wake in the early hours
and worry about Miss Pinkerton.
Letters for her are piling up in the hallway,
I think of her making an Irish stew
and forking an excellent dumpling.
I see her opening the wardrobe and saying no to a dress,
sex is not without a dose of stress.
What can a girl do with skin so pale?
Sometimes Miss Pinkerton runs naked from the bathroom
and cartwheels above my ceiling.

Sometimes I wake in the early hours
and ponder upon Miss Pinkerton.
Letters for her are piling up in the hallway,
I think of her eating a sticky pudding
and dabbing her eyes with a cucumber.
I see her opening her wardrobe and looking for leather,
I think Miss Pinkerton awfully clever.
What can a girl do with such Pre-Raphaelite hair?
Sometimes Miss Pinkerton runs naked from the bathroom
and sings Could You, Could You be Loved.

Sometimes I wake in the early hours
and contemplate Miss Pinkerton.
Letters for her are piling up in the hallway,
I think of her boiling a gorgeous ham
and throwing salt over her shoulder.
I see her opening the wardrobe and choosing a whip,
I think Miss Pinkerton a little hip.
What can a girl do with such libido?
Sometimes Miss Pinkerton runs naked from the bathroom
and taps upon my door like this

La Douceur de la Nuit

The refuse collectors
have been on strike for weeks.
I have never been so happy.

Bins have learnt to move
their hips. I've seen them
throbbing in the moonlight.

Have you heard
Cesária Évora's mournful song
to uncollected bins?

The rats link arms and
dance with melancholy
and the cats have

turned themselves
into aromatic troubadours.
When I open the window

pungent fruit leaps
onto my bed and the black sacks
sway like Belly Palms.